Program is both a basic aspect of architecture—the who, what, when, where, and why of a building or urban plan—and a powerful conceptual tool. FXFOWLE uses the matter-of-fact requirements provided by a client to reformulate basic architectural relationships and to drive innovation, efficiency, and building performance. Our challenge is to test the conventions of a program, applying them to create something new.

The design process puts forward an opportunity to analyze a client's mission and the way in which architecture can articulate it. Rethinking standard spatial relationships changes functionality. Various frameworks and different environments support contemporary approaches to work and learning and afford long-term flexibility.

Specific program requirements are vital to day-to-day operations and long-term success alike. Yet like any physical component of a building, the program may be crafted. Refining function and purpose contributes to design that has the power to do more: to achieve efficiency and generosity in combination; to offer more comfortable conditions for living, working, and learning; to enhance the intangible qualities that enrich a space; to define a sense of place.

We have found it vital to confront program in the context of new communications technologies. Wired connections are no longer necessary; job duties and collaborations can occur anytime and anywhere. The projects in this volume are flexible rather than rigid, innovative rather than strictly typological, effective rather than formulaic. Synergy between architecture and new paradigms for work and lear

At the **Hunter's Point Campus**, we have reinvented the traditional school typology to suit the urban context. The cafeteria is positioned on the top of the building to take advantage of views across the East River to Manhattan. The gym, at street level behind a translucent skin, integrates the building into its community. The new school landscape has the potential to change the way students think about their school.

The **Rockefeller Brothers Fund Offices** are an inversion of the typical office work place. The collaborative environment we have created facilitates productivity and presents a new public face for an organization that draws on the founding family's longstanding commitment to principled social change.

The **Columbia University School of Nursing** develops an energetic new identity for the school while fostering engagement with the surrounding community. A ribbonlike stair weaves its way through the building, emphasizing social interaction and connectivity. Simulation labs at the core of the building are surrounded by areas for work and study that epitomize a new approach to collaborative space.

At the **Golisano Institute for Sustainability** we have created a materials research laboratory that is integrated with the Rochester Institute of Technology campus. The mission of the institute—education and research into sustainability—is communicated through architectural expression and through design decisions that maximize natural lighting and limit artificial heating and cooling. The building is both site and showcase for sustainable environmental practices.

Positioned at the entrance to the Roswell Park Cancer Institute, the **Clinical Science Center** reconceptualizes the experience of arrival and at the same time satisfies requirements for clinical work and research. Positioned on a small but central site, the building clarifies circulation throughout the campus of the cancer center. Subtle environmental qualities—calm light, open views—encourage physical and psychological well-being in those undergoing treatment.

Smart, responsive, and efficient architecture operates to good effect. Rethinking and reformulating program relationships achieves tangible goals, such as building performance, as well as intangible ones: interaction and communication among users, aesthetics and civic identity. Reimagining purpose and function shows the power of design to influence not just the space itself but the ongoing and vital activities that take place within.

Effect: The Role of Program
Kim Tanzer

Kim Tanzer, FAIA is the Dean and Edward E. Elson Professor of Architecture at the University of Virginia School of Architecture.

Effect: to bring about. Effect: that which is brought about. Agent of change and result of change, subject and object, proactive and reactive: these aspects of effect play equivalent yet distinct roles in FXFOWLE's approach to program. The five projects here show that FXFOWLE has replaced the program as a given list of spaces with the program as an agenda that connects, asserts, mediates. This joyfully paradoxical program for architectural design pushes back against the basic parameters of the idea of program.

FXFOWLE's work, like that of most international, interdisciplinary firms, bears echoes of the waves of spatial planning methods that have prevailed over the past millenniums: site orientation, reinforcement of prevailing social norms, type-generated forms, and logistics of functional adjacencies. Yet FXFOWLE has moved beyond these historic practices to adjust form to changing uses.

The canonical texts of Western architecture all address the important role architects play in planning where to locate particular activities within buildings, how to assign activities to specifically designed and shaped spaces, and how to organize these spaces to make a whole. The architect is obligated to make these decisions evident to those who will use the building long after he or she departs.

Vitruvius, in the *Ten Books*, advocates a largely pragmatic approach to planning. Taking into account local geography and climate, he recommends placing functions to take advantage of natural elements and to protect against harsh conditions. He advises: "Winter dining rooms and bathrooms should have a southwestern exposure, for the reason that they need the evening light, and also because the setting sun, facing them in all its splendor but with abated heat, lends a gentler warmth to that quarter in the evening."[1]

Writing more than a millennium later, Leon Battista Alberti focuses on propriety and social relations as well as on physical practicalities. In describing a house for a gentleman, he recommends organizing spaces to indicate social hierarchy: "Each house . . . is divided into public, semi-private, and private zones . . . there should be no shortage of semi-private spaces,

1   **Vitruvius,** *The Ten Books on Architecture,* trans. Morris Hicky Morgan (New York: Dover Publications, 1960), 180–81.

walkways, promenades, swimming pools, areas both grassed and paved over, porticoes, and semicircular loggias, where old men may meet for discussion in the welcome winter sun, and where on holidays the family might pass the day, and where in summer grateful shade may be found."[2]

The concept of typology, the origins of which are thoughtfully articulated by Anthony Vidler in *The Writing of the Walls*, allows us to recognize a building's use by its massing, and to find our way through it because of its predictable organization.[3] Citing type studies of the eighteenth century, such as those of Durand and Ledoux, Vidler demonstrates the link between the proportions of a room and its location within a building using factories, hospitals, and prisons as case studies. The persuasive power of typology lies in its ability to render spatial arrangements legible and predictable. Typologies typically, and formulaically, align internal organization with external form.

Le Corbusier, too, took up the question of typology in his search for poetic generalities. At the same time he began to develop his theory of object-types, he famously asserted "the plan is the generator," capturing the sentiment that a building's organization and activities should fit like hand in glove. A plan is "an austere abstraction," he argued. "It is nothing more than an algebrization and dry-looking thing."[4] Le Corbusier asserted that buildings for manufacturing produced the most beautiful plans, because their logic of geometry was a direct response to their logic of use. While this focus on the plan led to sensitively designed spatial sequences, unique to each building's use, the one-to-one fit has, in the hands of less inventive designers, sometimes come to have a quality of formulaic inevitability.

This mechanistic, or functionalist, logic led in the 1960s to a specific approach to organizing interior relationships. Programming, as it came to be called, borrowed methods from the growing field of information design and held the promise of determining a preferred set of spatial relationships. The vestige of programming we carry with us today—a laundry list of rooms and square footages, often required by code—has created a legacy of oversized and uneconomically occupied buildings. Efficiency of thinking has not led to efficiency of use.

FXFOWLE has countered these legacies with inventiveness and sophistication. The Partners recognize that architecture must play an interpretive rather than a prescriptive role in structuring inhabitation and articulating ambition. At times they bend spatial organizations to reorder urban relationships; at other times their buildings are bent by local challenges. In many cases, the reconfiguration of internal relations may transform human interactions by presenting a "crystallized pedagogy," in the words of David Orr.[5]

We might think of FXFOWLE's approach to architecture as one that mediates between the public and the private, between the city and the individual, between the outside and

2   Leon Battista Alberti, *On the Art of Building in Ten Books*, trans. Joseph Rykwert, Neil Leach, and Robert Tavernor (Cambridge, Mass.: MIT Press, 1988), 145.

3   Anthony Vidler, *The Writing of the Walls: Architectural Theory in the Late Enlightenment* (New York: Princeton Architectural Press, 1987).

4   Le Corbusier, *Towards a New Architecture* (New York: Dover Publications, 1986), 180.

5   David Orr, "Architecture, Ecological Design, and Human Ecology," in *The Green Braid: Towards an Architecture of Ecology, Economy, and Equity*, ed. Kim Tanzer and Rafael Longoria (New York: Taylor & Francis, 2007), 15.

the inside. By taking on the role of shape shifter—rejecting type-driven organizations and style-driven forms—the office allows us to occupy the liminal space of now. The buildings provide a fluid connection between past expectations and future hopes, linking yesterday and tomorrow. FXFOWLE maintains that buildings are not objects but the manifestation, via various strategies, of a field of forces. The particular confluences FXFOWLE has developed are several, and they are deployed differently across a range of projects.

The Commons

Decades ago, the corridors of Bell Labs developed a reputation as the site of accidental meetings that led to research innovations. To build social connectivity and to prompt such exchanges, FXFOWLE implements large shared interior spaces, or centers and crossroads. Stairs also provoke chance encounters in a kind of vertical commons and promote exercise as well, improving occupants' health while reducing a building's energy footprint. The Golisano Institute for Sustainability at the Rochester Institute of Technology fuses these two forms in a central, daylit atrium. A shared stair connects multiple floors and is intended to prompt informal communications between researchers.

Icons

Geographers have long advocated the importance of imageable elements in buildings and in cities. These urban objects provide symbolic meaning and orientation. FXFOWLE uses icons to link buildings to larger contexts, especially urban ones, and to facilitate *wayfinding* and a sense of shared spatial identity. A key component of the Columbia University School of Nursing is a multi-story ribbon stairway visible from within the structure and from the street.

Transparency

Transparency serves several purposes for the firm. Offices and other rooms with external and internal window walls in effect expand the building's external membrane, inviting the outside deep within. Widespread access to daylighting indicates a concern for occupant health and well-being. Transparency—physical and visual—demonstrates an equalized social hierarchy and also symbolizes transparency in operations, an important element in creating an upstanding corporate culture. In the Rockefeller Brothers Fund Offices, a centrally located "grants hub" places the work of the organization in a physically and, by association, psychologically transparent location.

Beyond recurring formal elements, the architects' organizational kit of parts contains the qualities of optimism and precision, which inform the ways architectural components are deployed.

Optimism

The work of FXFOWLE evidences the conviction that strategic spatial moves can make a positive difference. The Hunter's Point Campus, designed for a tight site on the East River, takes advantage of spectacular views to Manhattan. Students observe this world-class vista, and imagine their future prospects in the great metropolis, from the top-floor cafeteria. The program has been adjusted to take full advantage of a stunning amenity that promises to inflect its young users' ambitions toward the limitless.

Precision

The office is noted for its carefully conceived massing and site orientation strategies, and for thoughtfully designed and well-detailed curtain walls and environmental systems. The Partners focus on reducing buildings' energy footprints and combining sustainable materials. They are equally conscientious in considering occupants' health, ease, sense of community, and creativity. The Clinical Science Center at the Roswell Park Cancer Institute confidently applies technical expertise and fine tuning to a program that encompasses clinical care, education, and research.

As the projects in this volume demonstrate, FXFOWLE is moving the concept of program beyond its modernist roots. The rigidity of type has been replaced by a fluid but familiar external and internal legibility. The deterministic plan has been replaced by a muscular realignment of spatial relations that prompts unexpected human interactions. The manipulation of best-case adjacencies has been replaced by supple and provocative spatial solutions. The prescriptive fit has been replaced by the loose fit, in which a hundred-year structure can accommodate myriad functions over its lifespan.

A new approach to program suggests a new kind of architect. FXFOWLE's efforts center less on controlling or manipulating behavior and more on suggesting actions. The firm's attention to the organization and pliability of spatial relationships serves local context, community goals, and changing uses and users. An effective implementation of program is the smart approach. Architecture is at best a partner in a dance; the building only rarely plays the leading role.

HUNTER'S POINT CAMPUS
QUEENS, NEW YORK, 2013
NEW YORK CITY SCHOOL CONSTRUCTION AUTHORITY
145,000 SQUARE FEET, NYC GREEN SCHOOL GUIDE COMPLIANT

We articulated the form of this building to sculpt a landscape, a dynamic design with high points, low points, ridges, and valleys. We want the students to feel like they are wrapped and embraced by the building.
Sylvia Smith

The new Hunter's Point Campus is a building shaped equally by its setting and by its program. We started with a simple volume determined by zoning regulations and the guidelines of the School Construction Authority, then carved from that volume to respond to views and neighborhood connections and to a reinterpreted program for the learning environment. The resulting form is both a civic landscape within the new neighborhood of Hunter's Point, Queens, and a school landscape with a coherent and bold identity.

The site for the school is adjacent to the new Hunter's Point South Waterfront Park and offers spectacular views to the East River and the Manhattan skyline. We inflected the normative boxy volume by carving slices out of the envelope. The ground level is recessed on the north and the south, defining distinct building entries. A granite base emerges from the ground plane and wraps up and around the exterior wall of the gym, anchoring the urban landscape.

Above the first floor, the building is clad in dark iron-spot brick with a sheen and tone that change dramatically in concert with the light of the day. Vibrant orange metal panels line the slices into the brick cladding. Two incisions mark the entrances, and two rise to sculpt a top-floor terrace, which reaches out to views west. An orange-clad swath of roof protects the open terrace area. A shaped brick parapet conceals mechanical equipment from the street.

Three programs within the building—high school, intermediate school, and special needs school—maintain individual identities through separate entry, circulation, classrooms, and administration areas. Special-needs classrooms are on the second floor, intermediate school classrooms on the third floor, and high school classrooms on the fourth and fifth floors. Corridors at each level are punctuated by windows within the exterior building incisions; these openings wash the hallways with natural light. Interior circulation is anchored by glass-enclosed stairs adjacent to the two entries. Movement within the building is brought to the exterior, animating the facade.

We distributed the larger program elements to generate a rich interior landscape. A typical facility positions the cafeteria, gym, and auditorium on the ground floor. Here they are situated to encourage students to move around and through the school. The ground-floor gym, which has a translucent wall assembly, connects to the neighborhood and to the public park across the street. The library, in the corner of the second floor, anchors the composition of the building with a wrapping of clear glass; this shared community space offers panoramic views. The auditorium occupies a central area on the third and fourth floors, poised between the intermediate and high schools. A faceted, orange shell, it produces an irregular landscape against the straight classroom blocks and registers the movement of students around it. On the fifth floor is the cafeteria. Shared by all students and faculty, the cafeteria expands to the adjacent terrace and its prospect over river and city. Artist Natasha Johns-Messenger created *Alterview*, a sixteen-by-ten-foot work of colored glass, to celebrate the terrace and its pride of place. This piece features a viewing portal to the skyline to the west.

The site and the program for the building offered opportunities not only for form but for investigation into the qualities that hew to any work of architecture: identity and cohesion. The institution as a whole and the independent learning environments within are distinct yet interwoven. At once solid and open, non-symmetrical and balanced, the unified figure of the school is energetic and active, not static. The orientation and configuration of the structure respond to intangible qualities of light and view as well as to tangible objectives; light in particular is an active element of the program. By creating a new experience of school within, for the students, Hunter's Point promotes a new understanding of school without, for the community and the city.

Main Entry

Library

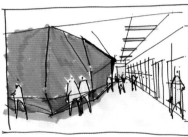

Corridors

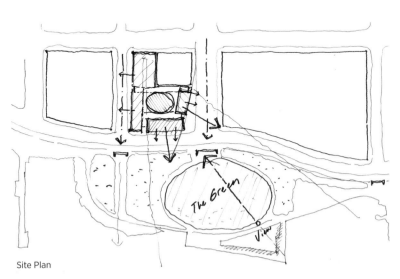

Site Plan

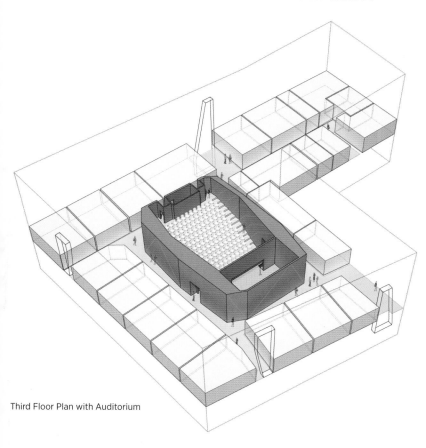

Third Floor Plan with Auditorium

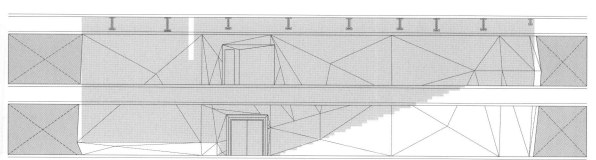

Auditorium Corridor Elevation

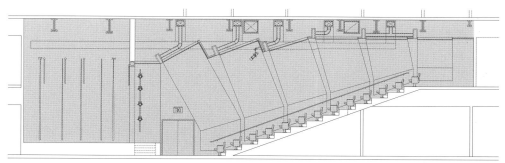

Auditorium Interior Elevation

This is the kind of project where it made sense to start with program exploration. We turned the organization inside out and rethought its grant-making process, developing a much more functional space that was flexible and wasn't locked into a single kind of use. Guy Geier

The Rockefeller Brothers Fund is a private family foundation that cultivates social change for a more just, sustainable, and peaceful world. It was organized by the children of John D. Rockefeller, Jr. as a vehicle through which they could share advice and research on charitable activities and coordinate their philanthropic efforts.

In 2005, with the lease on its Madison Avenue office about to expire, the fund decided to move to the Interchurch Center, a structure built in the 1950s by—coincidentally—the Rockefeller family as office space for not-for-profit organizations. Located on Riverside Drive in Upper Manhattan, the office looks out to Riverside Park, the Hudson River, and New Jersey's Palisades—a view preserved, in part, in the early twentieth century by the forward-thinking John D. Rockefeller, Jr. But the ceiling height was low, and the punched windows limited natural light and views.

The organization wanted the new office to offer a modern and comfortable working environment but also to support its values. Our flexible and open plan encourages communication, collaboration, and operational efficiency. The design strategy inverts the traditional office configuration. Private offices occupy the center of the floor plate; open work spaces surround the office core; large work and gathering areas are at the perimeter. We moved mechanical systems to the center of the floor plate to maximize the ceiling height at the perimeter, opening the office toward the view. Daylight penetrates all the way to the glass-walled private offices.

The communal spaces in the outermost zone of the office include the board room, café, and Grants Hub. At the old office, funding requests were passed from person to person and were often delayed along the way. We worked with the group to invent a new approach: the Grants Hub, the operational heart of the organization. Within the Grants Hub, each request, with related papers and files, is assigned a cubby; the staff reviews the grants in this central location. The old board room and its large, unwieldy table were used only for twice yearly board meetings. In the reimagined board room, we introduced modular tables that can be arranged in many configurations: for large and small meetings, training sessions, informal gatherings, individual stations, auditorium. A folding glass partition may be closed for acoustic privacy. The café, a pantry and small kitchen, supports board functions and staff lunches but also provides a social space for office celebrations and an informal area for meetings and conversation. It is populated with freestanding tables of various sizes, a banquette, and a bar.

Different types of furniture—from lounge chairs and coffee tables to barstools and counters—encourage many scenarios for working. Even file bays are at a height where they can be used as informal counters. Modular components facilitate varied configurations for specific requirements.

The relationship between workstations, offices, and informal work areas puts in place a structural flexibility that fosters a free and collaborative work environment.

To give employees and visitors an appreciation of Rockefeller history along with an understanding of the fund—what they were, are, and continue to be—many of our additions allude to the family's longstanding support for modern design and the arts. In the old offices, we discovered mid-century furniture, original but in disrepair. Restored pieces by Saarinen, Knoll, Mies, and others set the tone for the interior. In addition, on the Rockefeller family estate in the Hudson Valley, we came upon a pair of heavy wooden barn doors that had been in storage for years. We refinished the doors and placed them to each side of the main office entrance, creating a tangible connection to the family and to its historic property.

Efforts toward sustainability began with natural light. Dimming controls and occupancy sensors reduce the energy used for electric lighting. We updated the restrooms with low-flow toilets. At our suggestion, building management instituted bicycle parking and installed a white roof. The material palette includes materials with recycled content and low VOCs as well as those that are sustainably managed and rapidly renewable, such as FSC-certified woods and natural rubber.

Concept Sketch

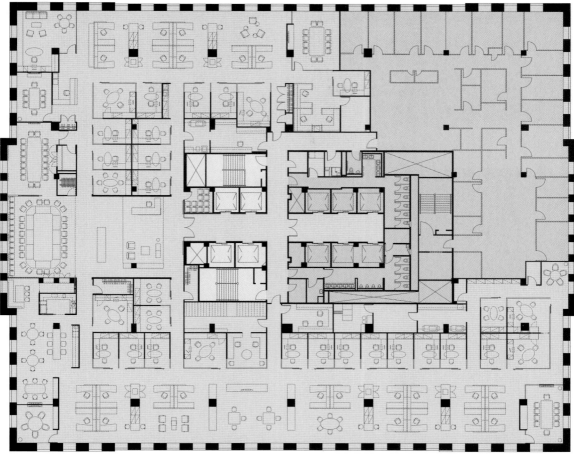

Plan

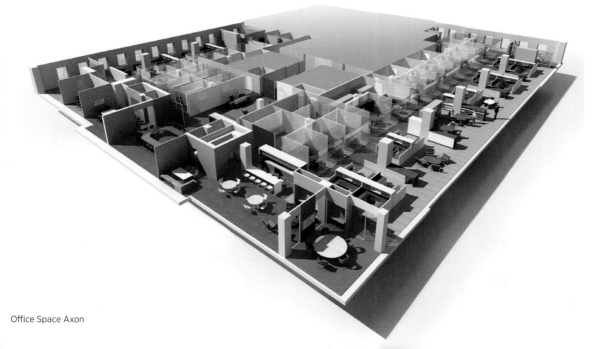

Office Space Axon

The form of the Golisano Institute is purposefully simple. It is a building designed entirely around daylight—a daylight diagram that creates a social hub for building users and for the campus. The building invites people to enter and to walk through.

Nicholas Garrison

The Golisano Institute for Sustainability is at the vanguard of education and research into sustainability across many disciplines—manufacturing, energy, mobility, information technology, and more. Our headquarters for the GIS is an advanced laboratory for scientific discovery and experiential learning. It facilitates the innovative technical and academic program of the institute with flexible "test bed" research labs, student work areas, classrooms and conference rooms, a sixty-five-seat auditorium, and office suites, all of which open onto a light-filled, four-story galleria.

While sustainable design is incorporated into all of our projects, the focus of the GIS demanded that we bring issues of sustainable execution and expression to the fore. The building is a living laboratory of sustainability where students, faculty, and visitors learn from how the building functions in response to the environment. Concepts of daylight drive the organization of the building, saving energy and improving indoor environmental quality at the same time. Transparency—in building materials and in access to both tangible space and intangible information—reveals the interrelationship between the sustainable systems of the building and the institute's research.

The GIS building is set on a former parking lot in the northwestern portion of the campus. The structure orders a fragmented area of the university, offers an opportunity for future expansion to the north, and forms a new gateway to the campus. It also encloses a generous new academic quadrangle. The east and west facades are solid brick, anchoring the building within the campus and minimizing sun exposure. The north and south facades—the two long facades—are composed of high-performance glass. The south face facilitates daylight harvesting, increasing solar gain in winter months; an aluminum sunshade system blocks the hot summer sun and mitigates glare. The north facade, modeled on early industrial loft buildings, overlooks the main approach to campus.

The building is composed of two shifted bars that form a central galleria. The four-story north bar is wider and contains the large test beds, mechanical spaces, and academic areas. The thinner south bar, three stories high, accommodates seminar and teaching rooms as well as academic and administrative offices and support areas. A large roof canopy spans the galleria, providing shade, unifying the overall composition, and affording the institute a distinct identity. The galleria, a threshold area and social space, links with and encloses part of the university's pathway system. A prominently placed staircase encourages socialization and invites users to bypass the elevator. The stair connects to a system of bridges, balconies, and translucent orange "learning pods" on the upper levels.

The galleria actively showcases learning and technology. Environmental performance data for the building, updated in real time, is displayed on an interactive electronic dashboard. A radiant floor system, which heats and cools the space, is supported by geothermal energy. Sensors and dampers govern air intake and exhaust; smoke purge equipment promotes ventilation. A passive environmental approach and solid enclosure systems help manage interior temperatures. The galleria is designed as a "buffer" zone that permits a more transitional climate with broader temperature swings. In winter, when temperatures can reach minus-twenty degrees outside, the galleria can reach a relatively balmy fifty-five. In summer, when it can be one hundred degrees outside, the interior temperature can approach about seventy-eight degrees.

This buffer zone can help to reduce the thermal loads on the interior surfaces of the program bars. The galleria admits natural daylight into every regularly occupied room in the building, minimizing artificial interior lighting.

The glazing technologies of the north and south walls enhance daylight penetration, offer campus views, provide robust insulation values, and allow for natural ventilation. Highly insulating translucent nanogel glazing brings natural light into the north and south bars; spandrel glazing furnishes additional insulation; vision glazing with radiant film technology, which conducts heat with a low-voltage charge, eliminates the need for perimeter heating; and glazing units with an internal suspended film impart the thermal performance of triple glazing.

Other sustainable design features include strategies for water use and energy production. A four-hundred-kilowatt fuel cell is a significant source of energy for the building. A microgrid system accepts power inputs from an on-site photovoltaic array, wind turbines, and microturbines. Components connected to the microgrid may be updated or entirely replaced as new technologies become available. Rain and snow that fall on the building's green roof will be released back to the environment through a rain garden and filtration system. The landscaped quadrangle defined by the building is an integral part of the water management system: water drains into the quad's catchment area and bioswales for reclamation by indigenous and noninvasive plantings.

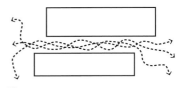

Flow

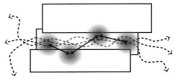

Activity

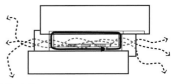

Circulation

Sustainable Strategies

1   Photovoltaic Panels

2   Green Roof

3   Wind Turbines

4   Solar Shading and High-Performance Insulated Glass

5   Chilled Beam Heating and Cooling

6   Steam and Chilled Water from Central Plant

7   Rainwater Harvesting and Cistern

8   Radiant Flooring and Ground-Source Heat Exchange

9   Air-Side Economizer Cycle

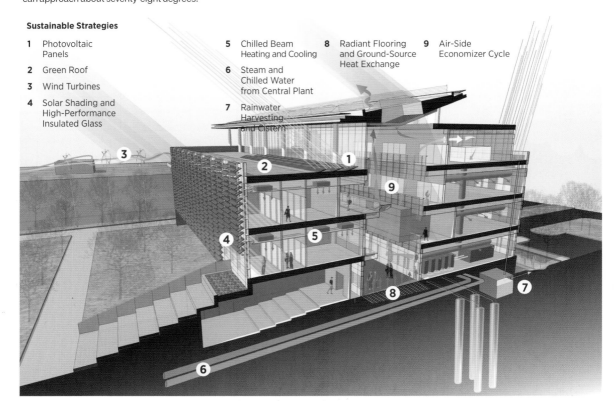

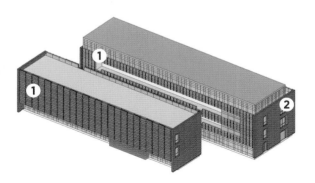

Building Components

1 Daylight Walls
2 Brick End Walls
3 Galleria Screens
4 South Screen
5 North Screen
6 Roof
7 Galleria

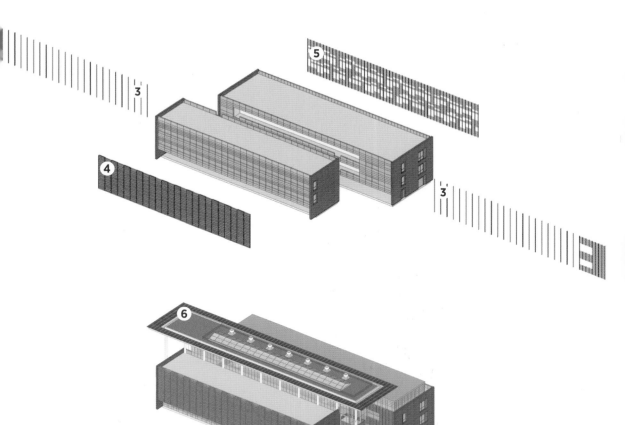

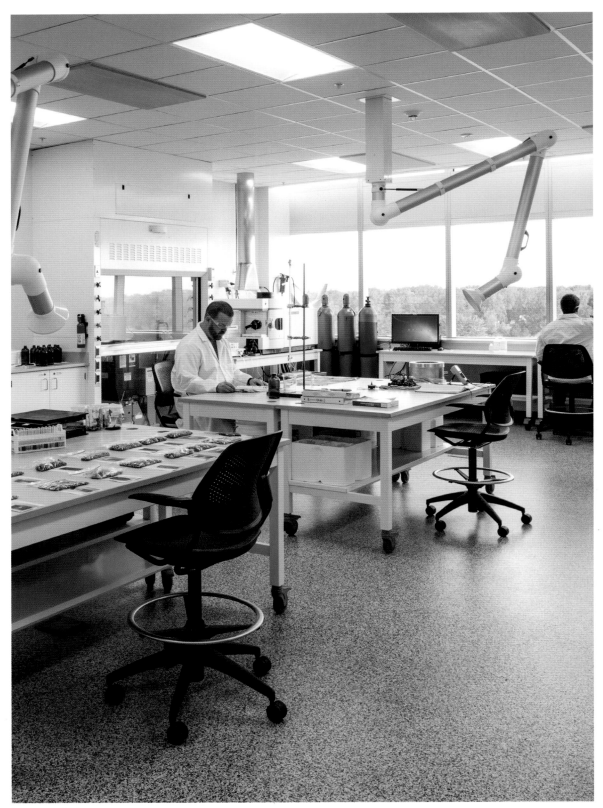

Battery Test Bed

Micro-turbine Test Bed

As we analyze a program, we do not take adopted standards at face value. We ask, How does your building really work? What is the amount of space you need to operate appropriately? It is a universal approach that allows for flexibility and growth and change.
Guy Geier

The Columbia University School of Nursing accommodates specialized functions—state-of-the-art simulation technology, research facilities, collaboration space, and student and faculty spaces—on the campus of the Columbia University Medical Center in the Washington Heights area of Manhattan. The school is densely programmed and alternates educational areas with spaces for community outreach. A "ribbon"—a stair that is visible from the street—weaves through the building and creates a distinct identity for the school.

The new building resulted from an invited design competition. The original brief called for a structure of three stories. Although zoning regulations permitted a larger building, the university administration wanted to preserve the air rights above the school for future expansion. Our competition entry instead proposed building to the full height allowed—seven stories—on half the site. By condensing the structure, we could make the nursing school more prominent and maintain a portion of the site for a future building. In addition, we were able to demonstrate that the compact footprint would be more suitable to the program and suggested that the school share the mechanical systems of the adjacent research building, achieving considerable cost savings.

We organized the building by stacking program elements in relation to requirements for public access and for natural lighting. Uses with connections to the public are placed on the lower floors; more specialized academic functions occupy the higher floors. Areas that need daylight are located at the perimeter, while controlled areas are at the core. The core and the perimeter, along with the ribbon stair, constitute three separate zones within the building. The whole is wrapped in a curtain wall of etched glass that admits diffuse light and creates a lantern effect for the building.

The ground floor invites the public to enter the school. The building lobby spills into a multipurpose community space that opens to the sidewalk. The ground floor also incorporates a gallery, student lounge and mailbox area, conference room, and student services including financial aid and admissions. The second and third floors provide simulation labs at the core and faculty offices, conference spaces, and student breakout spaces at the perimeter. The highly technical simulation labs, which mimic hospital patient and operating rooms, are the heart of the program. Configured in exactly the same way as those at hospitals and other medical facilities, they incorporate responsive mannequins and other sophisticated education technology.

Workstations and research spaces occupy the core on the fourth, fifth, and sixth floors. At the perimeter on the fourth floor, poised between community-oriented functions and internal academic programs, is the dean's office. Also on this level are a reception and conference area and offices for development and alumni relations. The fifth and sixth floors are ringed by faculty offices, conference

rooms, and breakout and study areas. On the uppermost level are a student lounge and terrace with green roof that will allow for special events with tremendous views of the city.

The ribbon stairway snakes through the building, uniting areas within the school, providing orientation from points inside and outside the building, and energizing the interior. Framed in glass and visible from the street, the ribbon emphasizes the building's verticality and highlights circulation as an organizing principle. A social space, the ribbon is linked to the various breakout and study areas.

The configuration of the building and allocation of spaces represent an understanding of how educational facilities have evolved. Offices are fairly small; support spaces—student study areas, unassigned conference rooms, and flexible research spaces—are larger, more plentiful, and can be arranged in multiple ways. Generated for workplace design, this disposition may be equally beneficial for advanced educational spaces, reinforcing a school's mission and pedagogy, facilitating collaboration, and encouraging online learning and group study.

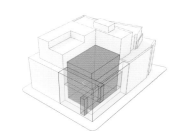

Organization

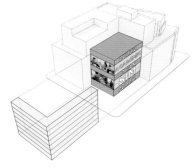

Program

Sim as Heart

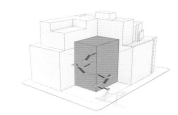

Circulation Ribbon

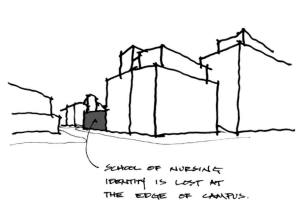

SCHOOL OF NURSING IDENTITY IS LOST AT THE EDGE OF CAMPUS.

Massing Proposed in Competition Brief

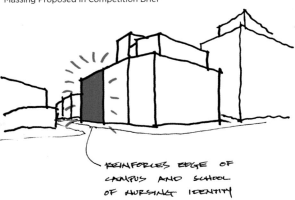

REINFORCES EDGE OF CAMPUS AND SCHOOL OF NURSING IDENTITY ON DAY ONE

Alternative Massing

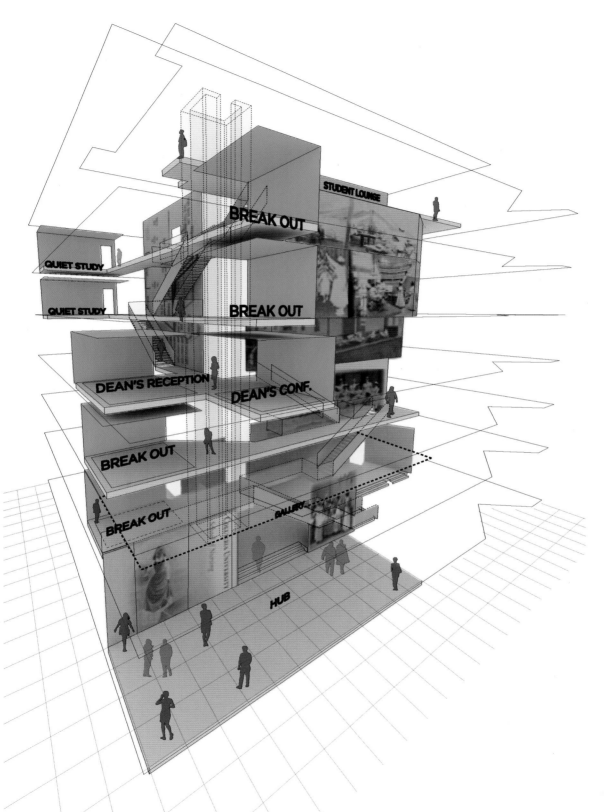

Circulation and Public Spaces

Columbia University
School of Nursing

Our design for Roswell Park reflects the best qualities of this storied institution. It strives to create a humane and uplifting environment for patients going through the arduous regimen of cancer treatment. It promotes the innovative work of researchers with its light-filled open design. And it seeks to create meaningful engagement with the larger context of Buffalo. Dan Kaplan

Founded in 1898 as the world's first laboratory for cancer research, Roswell Park Cancer Institute is a national leader in cancer care, research, and education. The main campus, located in downtown Buffalo, comprises fifteen buildings on twenty-five acres. The new Clinical Science Center is set on a tight but pivotal site at the main entrance to the complex. Supporting both clinical work and research, it offers a gateway to the institute that embodies and communicates its mission.

The eleven-story building is divided into two volumes, reflecting both solar orientation and programmatic content. A long serrated bar, which turns the corner from Michigan Avenue to Carlton Street, contains research and clinical functions arranged in cellular spaces. Set back on Carlton Street is a sleek glass tower with a canopy announcing the building entrance. This form houses larger, more public and communal spaces and responds to the southwestern orientation. We extracted uncommon utility from a highly constrained site. The Clinical Science Center connects to the main hospital and wraps around and cantilevers over an existing research facility, forming an inter-connected, three-dimensional composition.

The cladding systems respond to solar exposure and context. The east facade, with a curtain wall of glass and terra-cotta, is organized in a series of staggered bays; these "gills" are self-shading and maximize views in this portion of the structure. Rectangular and curved louvers within the curtain wall block sun exposure in certain areas while guiding natural light into the building in others. The sheer glass shaft admits daylight into the entrance atrium and ground-floor public areas. Protruding from this volume is a three-story "infusion box" with highlights of copper-mesh-embedded glass. The terra-cotta and copper hues reinforce the tonality of the Roswell Park campus (and nod to Louis Sullivan's nearby Guaranty Building) yet are modern and light.

The lower floors of the building are devoted to clinical space; the upper floors to offices. The infusion box, for those in chemotherapy, offers picturesque views of Buffalo's skyline and Lake Erie. The interior environment has been carefully tailored to provide physical and psychological comfort to patients receiving treatments, which can last several hours. The large glass surfaces are shaded by terra-cotta fins, reducing direct sunlight and glare; the effect will be a calm, even light. The infusion stations, configured with lounge-type seating, are arranged on a series of tiered platforms so that each patient has unobstructed views. The facility also houses an information center and patient library, a comprehensive breast services center that will provide screening mammography services, and administration and support areas. A conference center occupies the uppermost floor along with a terrace with pergola and a green roof.

We worked with the institute to reinvent the approach and entry to the campus around the new building. Visitors to Roswell Park arrive via Michigan Avenue, one of Buffalo's main north-south thoroughfares. But an extremely sharp turn onto Carlton Street, an elevated bridge that obscures the hospital entrance, and a recessed drop-off area add up to a less than welcoming experience. The entrance to the Clinical Science Center, positioned at the prominent intersection, signals not only the tangible presence of the institute but its ambitious calling.

Massing Principles

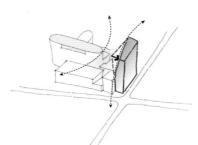

Inflect and Defer to Icons

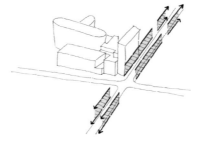

Address Michigan Avenue

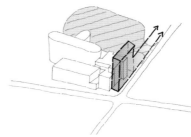

Screen Service Valley

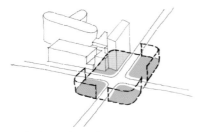

Facility Future Expansion

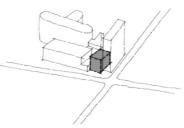

Create Public Space

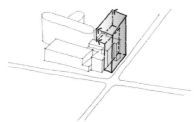

Cantilever Over Adjacent

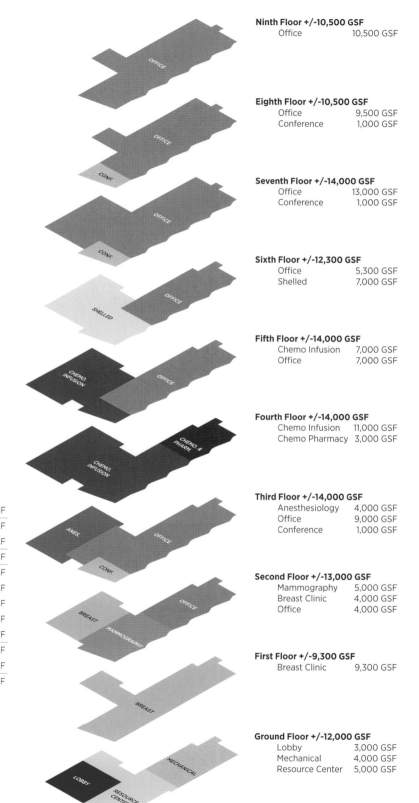

Ninth Floor +/-10,500 GSF
Office	10,500 GSF

Eighth Floor +/-10,500 GSF
Office	9,500 GSF
Conference	1,000 GSF

Seventh Floor +/-14,000 GSF
Office	13,000 GSF
Conference	1,000 GSF

Sixth Floor +/-12,300 GSF
Office	5,300 GSF
Shelled	7,000 GSF

Fifth Floor +/-14,000 GSF
Chemo Infusion	7,000 GSF
Office	7,000 GSF

Fourth Floor +/-14,000 GSF
Chemo Infusion	11,000 GSF
Chemo Pharmacy	3,000 GSF

Third Floor +/-14,000 GSF
Anesthesiology	4,000 GSF
Office	9,000 GSF
Conference	1,000 GSF

Second Floor +/-13,000 GSF
Mammography	5,000 GSF
Breast Clinic	4,000 GSF
Office	4,000 GSF

First Floor +/-9,300 GSF
Breast Clinic	9,300 GSF

Ground Floor +/-12,000 GSF
Lobby	3,000 GSF
Mechanical	4,000 GSF
Resource Center	5,000 GSF

Schematic Program

Mechanical	4,000 GSF	
Conference	3,000 GSF	
Office	58,300 GSF	
Shelled	7,000 GSF	
Chemo Pharmacy	3,000 GSF	
Chemo Infusion	18,000 GSF	
Anesthesiology	4,000 GSF	
Mammography	5,000 GSF	
Breast Clinic	13,300 GSF	
Resource Center	5,000 GSF	
Lobby	3,000 GSF	
	123,600 GSF	

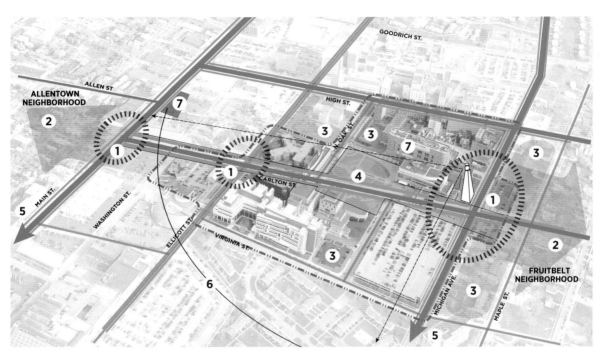

Campus Opportunities

1   Create Beacon and Campus Gateways

2   Connect to Neighboring Communities

3   Propose Potential Expansion Sites

4   Create Green Corridor

5   Strengthen Connection to Downtown via Michigan Avenue and Main Street

6   Offer Views Toward Skyline and Lake Erie

7   Improve Connection to Main Street and Transit

Massing Studies

Infusion Box

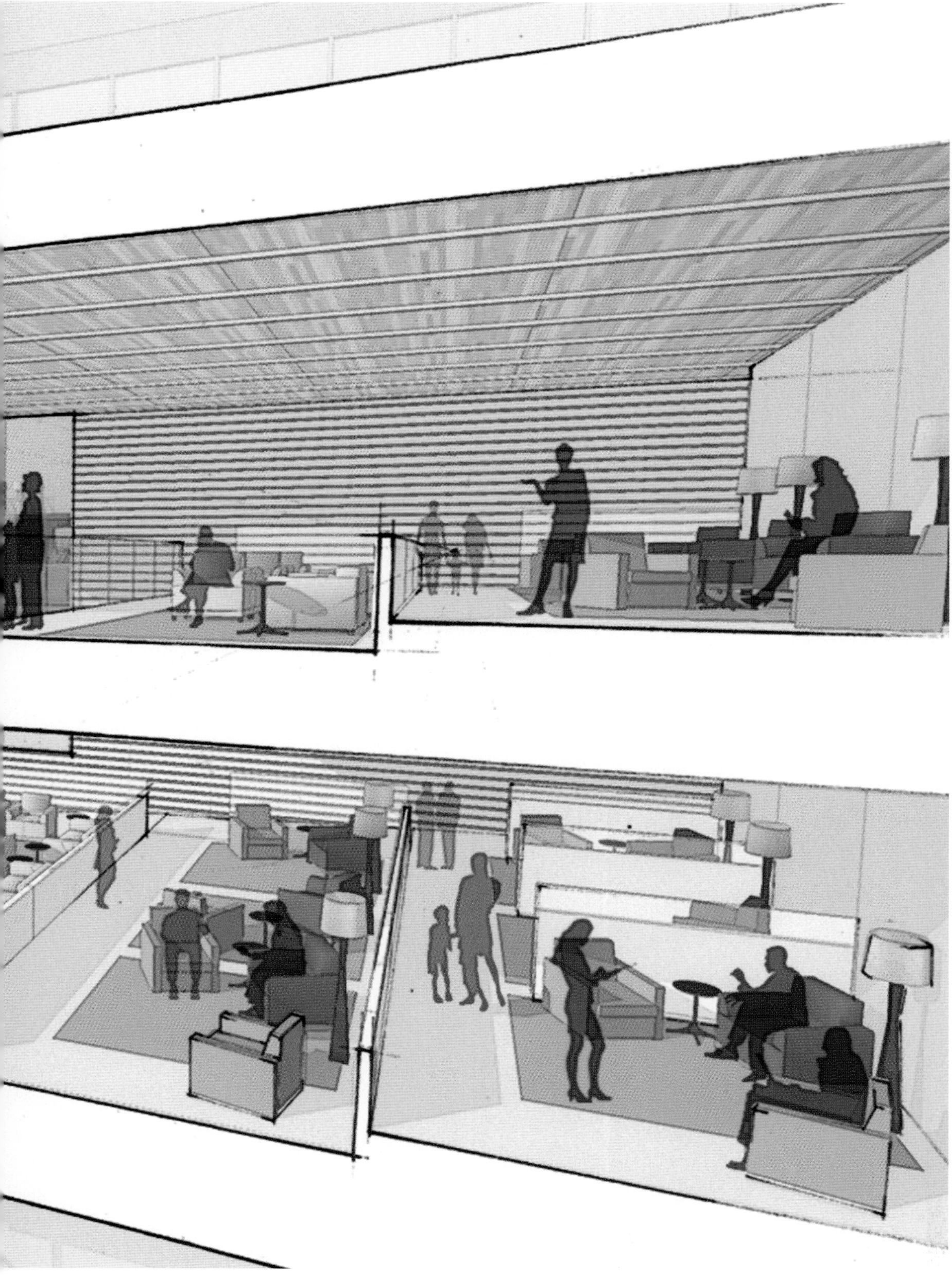

Senior Partners
Gerard F. X. Geier II, FAIA, FIIDA, LEED
Sudhir S. Jambhekar, FAIA, RIBA, LEED
Daniel J. Kaplan, FAIA, LEED
Sylvia J. Smith, FAIA, LEED
Mark E. Strauss, FAIA, AICP/PP, LEED

Partners
Heidi L. Blau, FAIA, LEED
Tim Milam, AIA, LEED
John Schuyler, AIA, LEED

Founding Principal
Bruce S. Fowle, FAIA, LEED

Project Credits

Introduction/Effect

Golisano Institute for Sustainability,
Gene Avallone (p2), Coe Hoeksema (p6),
David Lamb (p8)
Rockefeller Brothers Fund Offices,
Eric Laignel (p10)
Hunter's Point Campus,
David Sundberg/Esto (p12),
Coe Hoeksema (p14)

Hunter's Point Campus

Partner-in-Charge: Sylvia Smith
Project Director: Ann M. Rolland
Project Architect, Project Manager:
Timothy Macy, Mark Nusbaum,
Eric Van Der Sluys
Project Designer: Nicholas Garrison,
William Haskas
Team: Kazuhiro Adachi, Gregory
Chann, MyPhuong Chung, Aaron
Dai, Violette de la Selle, Adam Fisher,
Fernanda Freitas, Miwa Fukui, Dawn
Hood, Illiana Ivanova, Jiyoung Lee,
Heng-Choong Leong, Scott Melching,
Gerard Sambets Jr., Stephanie
Schreiber, Gerardo Sustaeta

Structural Engineer: Ysreal A. Seinuk, PC
MEP, Fire Protection Engineer:
Kallen & Lemelson, LLP
Site, Civil, Landscape, Geotechnical
Engineer: Langan Engineering,
Environmental, Surveying and
Landscape Architecture, D.P.C.
A/V, Acoustical: Cerami & Associates, Inc.
Lighting: Tillotson Design Associates
Elevator: Van Deusen & Associates
Food Service: Romano Gatland
Photography: David Sundberg/Esto

Rockefeller Brothers Fund Offices

Partner-in-Charge: Guy Geier
Project Manager: Erica Godun
Project Designer: Daniel Jacoby
Team: Sara Agrest, Violette de la Selle,
Stephanie Schreiber, Joseph White

Owner's Representative:
Levien & Company
MEP Engineer: Cosentini Associates
Structural Engineer:

Gilsanz, Murray, Steficek
Construction Manager:
John Gallin & Son
Lighting: Illumination Arts LLC
A/V, Acoustical: Cerami & Associates
Commissioning Agent: Joseph R.
Loring & Associates
Photography: Eric Laignel

Golisano Institute for Sustainability

Partner-in-Charge: Dan Kaplan
Project Director: John Schuyler
Project Architect: Steve Mielke
Design Principal: Nicholas Garrison
Senior Designer: Gustavo Rodriguez
Team: Jason Abbey, Kazuhiro Adachi,
Max Carr, Violette de la Selle,
Miwa Fukui, Brandon Massey,
Joseph Pikiewicz

Construction Manager: Lechase
Construction Services
Architect of Record, Structural
Engineer, Landscape Architect:
SWBR Architecture, Engineering
& Landscape Architecture, P.C.
Civil Engineer: Stantec
MEP Engineer: M/E Engineering, P.C.
Photography: David Lamb

Columbia University School of Nursing

Partner-in-Charge: Guy Geier,
Scott Kelsey*
Project Manager, Project Architect:
Michael Syracuse
Project Designer: Nicholas Garrison
Team: Amanda Abel, Kazuhiro Adachi,
Jonathan Coble, Miwa Fukui, Christina
Galati, Ilana Judah, Jonathan Kanda*,
Munhee Kang, Jatin Kayastha*,
Alvaro Quintana
*CO Architects staff

Architect: CO|FXFOWLE Architects LLC
MEP, Fire Protection Engineer: AKF Group
Structural Engineer: DeSimone
Consulting Engineers
Geotech, Site, Civil Engineering:
Langan Engineering, Environmental,
Surveying and Landscape
Architecture, D.P.C.
A/V, Acoustical, Vibration: Cerami

& Associates, Inc.
Code: Code Consultants Professional
Engineers, PC
Curtain Wall, Exterior Wall: Axis
Facades USA, LLC
Cost Estimating: Toscano
Clements Taylor
Lighting: Office for Visual Interaction, Inc.
Security: Aggleton and Associates
Vertical Transportation: Van Deusen
& Associates
Wind/Air Dispersion: Rowan
Williams Davies and Irwin Inc.
Facade Maintenance: Entek Engineering
Traffic: Sam Schwartz Engineering, PLLC
Signage: Calori & Vanden-Eynden
Design Consultants
Expeditor: Milrose Consultants, Inc.
Construction Manager:
TDX Construction Corporation

Clinical Science Center

Partner-in-Charge: Daniel Kaplan
Project Manager: Daniel Schmitt,
John Schuyler
Job Captain: Scott Melching
Project Architect: Daniel Schmitt
Project Designer: Daniel Kaplan,
Brandon Massey
Team: Kazuhiro Adachi, Fernanda
Freitas, Miwa Fukui, Marti Gottsch,
Ervin Hirsan, Hyung Kim, Heng-
Choong Leong, Joseph Pikiewicz,
Valeria Rivera Deneke, Gerardo
Sustaeta, Sisto Tallini, Seiji Watanabe,
Jiehan Yang

Structural Engineer: Severud Associates
Mechanical Engineer: Watts
Architecture and Engineering
Electrical Engineer: Buffalo Engineering
Civil Engineer: C&S Companies
Facade: Axis Facades
Facade Maintenance: Entek Engineering
Architectural Lighting: One Lux Studio

Published by
ORO Editions
Publisher: Gordon Goff
Copyright © 2014 by FXFOWLE Architects, LLP
ISBN: 978-1-935935-63-6
10 09 08 07 06 5 4 3 2 1 First Edition

Consulting Editor: Andrea Monfried
Text: Liz Campbell Kelly
Design: ORO Editions
FXFOWLE Monograph Team: Guy Geier, Amanda Abel, Karen Bookatz, and Brien McDaniel
Color Separations and Printing: ORO Group Ltd.
Production: Usana Shadday and Alexandria Nazar
Printed in China

This book was printed and bound using a variety of sustainable manufacturing processes
and materials including aqueous-based varnish, VOC- and formaldehyde-free glues, and
phthalate-free laminations. The text is printed using offset sheetfed lithographic printing
process in 5 color on 140 gsm woodfree art paper and 157 gsm matt art paper with an off-line
spot gloss varnish applied to all photographs.

ORO Editions makes a continuous effort to minimize the overall carbon footprint of its
publications. As part of this goal, ORO Editions, in association with Global ReLeaf, arranges
to plant trees to replace those used in the manufacturing of the paper produced for its books.
Global ReLeaf is an international campaign run by American Forests, one of the world's
oldest nonprofit conservation organizations. Global ReLeaf is American Forests' education
and action program that helps individuals, organizations, agencies, and corporations improve
the local and global environment by planting and caring for trees.

Library of Congress Cataloging-in-Publication Data:
Available upon request